This Book Belongs To

Made in the USA
Monee, IL
19 May 2025

17752858R00063